OVERCOME &
Rise Above

SECOND EDITION

HOW TO TURN THE DOWNSIDE OF CHALLENGES INTO THE UPSIDE OF RENEWING YOUR LIFE

MICHELLE WATSON

Breakfree Forever Publishing

Copyright © Michelle Watson
2ND edition

ALL RIGHTS RESERVED. No part of this book may be reproduced or transmitted in any form whatsoever, electronic, or mechanical, including photocopying, recording, or by any informational storage or retrieval system without the expressed written, dated and signed permission from the author.

Author: Michelle Watson
Title: Overcome & Rise Above
ISBN: 978-1-7384171-2-4
Category: SELF-HELP/Personal Growth/General
Publisher: Breakfree Forever Publishing

LIMITS OF LIABILITY / DISCLAIMER OF WARRANTY: The author and publisher of this book have used their best efforts in preparing this material. The author and publisher make no representation or warranties with respect to the accuracy, applicability, or completeness of the contents. They disclaim any warranties (expressed or implied), or merchantability for any particular purpose. The author and publisher shall in no event be held liable for any loss or other damages, including but not limited to special, incidental, consequential, or other damages. The information presented in this publication is compiled from sources believed to be accurate, however, the publisher assumes no responsibility for errors or omissions. The information in this publication is not intended to replace or substitute professional advice. The author and publisher specifically disclaim any liability, loss, or risk that is incurred consequently, directly, or indirectly, of the use and application of any of the contents of this work.

Printed in the United Kingdom

OVERCOME & Rise Above

SECOND EDITION

HOW TO TURN THE DOWNSIDE OF CHALLENGES INTO THE UPSIDE OF RENEWING YOUR LIFE

MICHELLE WATSON

Breakfree Forever Publishing

TABLE OF CONTENTS

Foreword   9
Introduction   11

CHAPTER 1 | *The Beginning*   15
CHAPTER 2 | *My Journey*   25
CHAPTER 3 | *Get Rid of Fear*   33
CHAPTER 4 | *Forget the Disappointments and Shame*   43
CHAPTER 5 | *What is your Diagnosis?*   53
CHAPTER 6 | *Let Go of Resentment and Hurt*   61
CHAPTER 7 | *Perseverance*   69
CHAPTER 8 | *Don't Be Proud — Seek Help*   75
CHAPTER 9 | *Live Solutions, Not Problems*   83
CHAPTER 10 | *Hope, Positive Speaking and Mindset*   87

Conclusion   99
Resources The Author Recommends   101
Acknowledgement   103
Bonus Chapter   105

This book is dedicated to the loving memory of my grandfather, 'Shilo' Clarence Sinclair. I want to also dedicate my story to all parents anywhere in the world, particularly the United Kingdom and the Caribbean, who are challenged daily by nurturing and raising children faced with disabilities such as attention deficit hyperactivity disorder (ADHD). This dedication would be incomplete if I did not include Santana, Rashaun, and Alisha, my wonderful gifts of life and love.

FOREWORD

This book *Overcome And Rise Above: How To Turn 7e Downside Of Your Challenges Into the Upside Of Renewing Your Life* provides a series of guidelines, examples and spiritual perspectives for making sure that as parents and individuals, you have the right tools to ensure future success in facing your challenges. The book highlights contructive points on not only issues surrounding ADHD but also various challenges concerning abuse and the many troubles that individuals face throughout their life journeys. It is a book full of hope and determination, giving you the chance to see that after a storm there can sometimes be calm. It provides a powerful comparison between various circumstances faced when you have been labelled and segregated from others. Reading it will give you the willpower to continue and not give up.

James MacNeil

Author of the *Guru Builder*
Website: *www.thegurubuilder.com*
Email: *james@eqcommunications.com*
Twitter: *www.twitter.com/jamesmacneil*
Tel. No.: +1 416 840 0625

In our generation, many people love sitting on a bench of regret, thinking about how badly life has treated them, whilst others are taking charge of their lives and pushing through barriers to turn their obstacles into golden opportunities. After reading this book, I knew in my heart that this young, dynamic woman is a true example of how one can rise above one's challenges.

No purpose can be achieved easily, and everyone who wants to live a purposeful life must go through challenges. The obstacles you face will determine your purpose in life. The only person that loses out on life's benefits is one who refuses to do anything in the midst of challenges. As Michelle Watson has highlighted, if there is no mess, there will definitely be no message. I implore everyone to follow all the rich advice inside this book, as it is enough to get anyone through the wilderness of life. Happy reading!

Ptr. Peter Oyebobola

Author of *7e Power of Choice and How to Acquire Money*
Website: www.praisetek.co.uk
Email: praisetek@hotmail.com
Tel. Nos.: +44 7961 193 137
Twitter: www.twitter.com/praisetek
Skype: peter.Oyebobola

INTRODUCTION

Most people do not realise the effects and huge challenges that raising a child with a disability has on a family. The emotions, hurt, burdens, lasting thoughts and vicious roller-coaster ride.

I wrote this book because I have had this experience and thought writing about it might encourage someone facing one challenge or another in their lives. I will address challenges with my son who has ADHD (attention deficit hyperactivity disorder), as well as some personal issues of my own. The book aims to enlighten many about these difficulties.

I am aware that some readers of this book may not be Christians, religious, or even believe in God. However, as a Christian, I have learnt much that I was able to apply in my challenges; I do hope that these lessons can also be of some help to you. What I say to people is to forget about labelling or dwelling on the statements of 'I believe' or 'don't believe'. Instead look at the benefits, possibilities, and the morals of what you wish to achieve.

I would implore you to consider seriously some of what I have discussed, as I have been open and honest, though doing so was not easy.

I can only share with you what I have experienced and what did or didn't work for me. As I have highlighted in the book, not everything will apply or work for you, but I have no doubt that after reading this book you will have a new mind-set and attitude in your approach to challenges, the way you view parents of children who have ADHD, or even the way you view the children themselves. As you read this book, I believe you will gain an insight into the hearts of people facing challenges and come across things you would have never thought that an individual would be feeling. We all see parents going about their daily lives, running errands, going to work, being housewives, and husbands or struggling with their children on the bus, in the shops or streets. We cast judgements without knowing anything about what is going on in the lives of these individuals. I hope that after reading, you may change whatever mind-set you have developed relating to this matter. Surprisingly, there is a lot you can learn about yourself by reading about the lives of others; this book may be just the eye-opener for you to make a difference not only in your life but the lives of your family and those around you.

For those of you who decided to read this book in spite of not facing any of the challenges addressed, I do hope that it will make you become aware of the challenges others face and realise how grateful you should be for not having to face these issues. Parents, be encouraged. You are not on your own. There are a lot of other mothers and fathers out there who are facing the same or similar difficulties as you. Take comfort in knowing that others have overcome, and that can you as well; overcome the challenges that are faced in the journey of a mother's heart.

1
The Beginning

"All great deeds and all great thoughts have a ridiculous beginning. Great works are often born on a street corner or in a restaurant's revolving door."

— *Albert Camus*

* * *

The phone rings and my heart skips a beat; it's the school. My mind goes into turmoil, what has gone wrong now: What has he done? Is this one more exclusion? I ignore the first, second and third rings. Then it stops. I pick up the phone to return the call. The secretary answers and when I tell her who it is, she quickly says 'it's nothing to worry about'–she was only calling to remind me of a meeting that was scheduled in the next few days. I let out a sigh of relief, thanking God that's all it was. I don't know if you have ever had that experience of hearing your phone ringing and dreading what you're going to hear on the other end of the line.

In order to give you clear understanding, let me start from the beginning. God has blessed me with three beautiful children: Two gorgeous girls, Santana and Alisha, and a handsome boy, Rashaun. My son, however, has been since the age of two what they call 'a handful'.

He was born in July, 2003 after a difficult pregnancy during which I was hospitalised twice. His delivery was very difficult and lasted the duration of 16 hours before I was given an emergency caesarean because he became distressed. My son had to be kept in the intensive care unit in North Middlesex Hospital for five days; he had taken in meconium (a substance from his excrement) and got infected so had to be fed by a tube through his nostrils. It was a challenging time, being worried and not knowing what to do. I was as any normal mother would be–in a state of confusion. Since then, it has been an uphill battle with many complications, meetings, hair-pulling situations and, of course, happy moments too.

I first realised my son's journey was not normal when he reached the age of two. He would stand on the bed, or any tall edge he could reach, and jump off; it seemed as if there was absolutely no fear in him. One night, after having his bath, three-year-old Rashaun climbed onto the top of the bath and jumped off, hitting his mouth on the edge of the tub. I was so scared, seeing all that blood. I rushed him to the hospital, where he had the wound glued shut.

I remembered the nurse asking me in an accusing voice how I could have allowed that to happen. I was in tears, thinking to myself, this nurse has no idea what I am going through.

Rashaun used to have the wildest tantrums and got into rages so bad that it was as if he no longer knew who he was. Once, at the age of three, he got so angry that he shattered a mirror on the front of a wardrobe I had in the bedroom; I was so shocked that the memory still lingers in my head just as if it were only yesterday. 'I know where I have seen this behaviour before', I said to myself, but I kept thinking, he is only a boy and he will grow out of it, or I would say 'it's just the age of the terrible twos'. But stop and think about that phrase: Why would you want to call your child the negative label of a 'terrible two'?

I was born in Enfield in north-east London and currently live in Tottenham. At the age of three I re-located to Westmoreland, Jamaica with my maternal grandparents, Hazel and Clarence Sinclair. I first became pregnant in Jamaica with my eldest daughter, Santana, in 2000 and decided to return to the UK, believing it would be much easier to be surrounded by more of the family. After a while in England, I was feeling very lonely, despite having a big family around me: It was as though I was in search of comfort and reassurance — and then he showed up, offering all the love a young woman could dream of having! Looking back, I believe I just wanted to fill an emotional void. He ticked all the boxes of just the kind of man that I wasn't looking for ... but I fell just the same, as he came at a very low point in my life.

My eldest daughter was one year old when I met him, and she bonded with him almost immediately, as he was so kind and lovely, taking every opportunity he had to give us enjoyment. We decided to move in together, and shortly after that we got married. I was four months pregnant at the time, and slowly after that, things started to change for the worse.

As I said, before we lived together he was loving, caring, very good with my daughter and liked cooking. But he was like Jekyll and Hyde; one side of him he had an anger like no other. The abuse that came from his mouth would make you cringe to the depths of your soul. I experienced both physical and mental abuse from him, both so bad that it became a joy to be at work and felt like the end of the world to return home. He would complain and start arguments about of the smallest situations. I lost all self-esteem and could feel the life, joy and happiness that I once knew drain away from me.

I saw him display such blind anger that he would destroy things, smashing furniture, a television, and then say the nastiest filth. I was filled with terror. He would cry about it after he had calmed down and saw what he had done. He would apologise, pleading with me to forgive him and I would give him another chance, which happened over and over again. I was cut off from my friends, as there was always an issue when I went out with them or even visited their houses.

> *This is where we go wrong: always trying to change what we cannot instead of focusing on what we can change.*

* * *

One night we both wanted to go out with our friends the same night I did, and he told me I couldn't go. At this point I hid from him when I went out, so as soon as he left that night, I went out and came back home before he did–but he found out the following morning. At the time I had a benign tumour, a massive lump that was growing behind my left ear, and without hesitation or thought he punched me right on the area where the lump was. The pain was excruciating the next day, and my face as well as my neck was swollen. I couldn't let my family know what was happening to me: I was worried about the mayhem it would have caused, and the failure I would appear to be.

This is what domestic abuse does to you–it makes you think that it is entirely your fault that you have failed. How could I explain to anyone what I was going through? At what point could I open my mouth and say the words? This was the greatest challenge for me at this point. Me? Michelle, from a well-known family, a happy-go- lucky and cheerful young woman, having food thrown in my face and lowered by words that made me feel like scum, being kicked and disgraced in public?

I was put down to his friends, shouted and sworn at in supermarkets, humiliated on the street–the list never ended. I would tell myself, this is not me; the Michelle I know would never take this, but on the other hand I kept holding on to the hope that I could change him somehow. This is where we go wrong: Always trying to change what we cannot instead of focusing on what we can change.

I finally came to the realisation that it was the wrong atmosphere for the children. Rashaun at the time was three and Santana was five. It was heart-breaking for the kids and for me as well. I felt like I was a failure: In my early twenties, I was already divorced and had two children of different fathers. No matter how hard I tried, I started to think that I was the problem.

I know that some of you in the same position can understand what I am saying: That feeling of shame and embarrassment when you have to disclose at some point that your children are not from the same dad, especially when you know that you are not someone that sleeps about or the one who was at fault for the end of the relationship.

However, I'm here to tell you to get rid of the self-pity and be proud of yourself. Learn to forgive yourself for any mistakes you may have made in the past so that you can allow yourself to move forward. As Paul urged in the Philippians 3:13: 'Brothers, I do not consider that I have made it my own. But one thing I do; forgetting what lies behind and pushing forward to what lies ahead'. I had to move forward, and I felt I had to make that drastic decision before I lost my life and anymore of my sanity, even if it meant becoming a single parent bringing up two children on my own.

I felt so confused and unsure of what my next step should be. I did know that I had a difficult task ahead of me, but how difficult I did not know. I had reached a point of no return. I had made a choice and, as you know, the choices you make determine what your future is going to be. I told myself that no matter what lies ahead, I'll have to be strong, if not for me at least for my children: If I couldn't be, then who would?

Mothers especially always have the perspective, 'I have kids so I can't' instead of saying, 'because I have children, I have to'. Robert Kyiosaki opened my eyes to this in his book called *Rich Dad, Poor Dad*. The fact that you have become a parent does not mean that there is a limit to your success. Instead of using it as an excuse to fail, use it as a drive to succeed. People always ask me how I do it: Work, write a book, run to all the meetings and also be a church volunteer. You decide your destiny, and you are the potter with the ability to design your clay the way you want it. Many of us mothers tend to feel on our own at our lowest points. At that time, I would crawl into a shell like a turtle, leaving out just enough of my head to do my basic daily duties for the kids before returning into hiding. Tears were my pillow; they woke me up in the mornings and put me to bed at night.

I felt like all hope had gone yet the children, as innocent as they were, still wanted to have fun, go to the park or play games like the other children in the neighbourhood, all I wanted to do was lie in my bed and pull the sheets over my head. Phillipians 4:13 says, 'I can do all things through Christ who strengthens me…' This was (and still is) one of the many passages that kept me going through the tough years. I knew that what was coming wouldn't be easy and despite my determination to press forward, there did come times when I felt like giving up. But no matter the circumstances, I urge you to keep telling yourself that there will be light at the end of the tunnel. Reciting this verse will help you to keep calm and give you peace of mind in knowing that victory is sure. This low point was also the beginning of a new era for me in which I would experience love, disappointment, discouragement, hope, laughter, tears and all the pain a mother's heart could experience. It was the beginning also because of what my pastor once told me: After every full stop there is a capital letter, a new beginning and a new challenge.

What i learnt is that with every circumstance there is an end, and after that end is another beginning.

* * *

What I learnt is that with every circumstance there is an end, and after that end is another beginning, another issue to face and another problem to solve. Everyone going through similar low points in your lives should take heart and keep on smiling, because you are not on your own. I can now look back and say to myself, and to all of you, that I never thought it would have been possible to make it this far, but with steel-like determination and the grace of God I did and so can you. In the next chapters, I will share my experience and the story of my heart.

SEND AN EMAIL FOR A FREE 30-MINUTE ONE-ON-ONE
"BREAKTHROUGH FROM FEAR" CLARITY SESSION.
MICHELLEWATSON@BREAKFREEMW.COM

2
My Journey

"Sometimes it's the journey that teaches you a lot about your destination."

— *Drake*

* * *

My mother, Anita, is the third child of my grandparents, Hazel and Shilo Sinclair, who raised me. I was born in 1981 to Anita and Colin Smith, but a year after I was born, my mother and father separated, so I spent more time with my grandparents than with my mother as she worked long hours. My grandfather was involved in a major car accident and lost his sight in his eye, which affected him drastically. Granddad was a party animal, very outgoing, funny, all the ladies' choice; one you would call a 'hot shot'. You couldn't be around granddad and have a sombre face. It just couldn't happen.

They made the decision to move back to Jamaica in 1984, and I went with them. Because I was coping so well in Jamaica, it was decided that I should remain there and be brought up by my grandparents. I am sure it must have been difficult for my mother to decide to allow her only child to live so far from her, but she visited me every six months and spoke to me as often as she could.

As the time went by, the feeling of loneliness crept up on me, since I was the only family member living with my grandparents. There were times when other cousins came to stay with us for lengthy periods, but they didn't stay. I was well cared for but felt left out like I wasn't a part of the family. Don't get me wrong: The rest of the family in the UK never left me out. They always ensured what all the other cousins received, I got as well, but to me it just wasn't the same. My aunties were and still are amazing. During my childhood they made yearly visits, and I developed a wonderful relationship with my cousins from London. There was one downside to this–they didn't know, but the inevitable time to say 'goodbye' after Christmas was dreadful for me.

There were times I felt like I had neither mother nor father, especially when an astronomical rise in the cost of air travel caused my mother to visit less frequently. I was also anxious to know my siblings, and I had a dad with whom I still had no communication. It was becoming more difficult to handle a number of challenges as I was getting older and couldn't speak to my grandparents about certain things. My grandmother was very strict; granddad, on the other hand, was more approachable, but wasn't someone I could approach to discuss teenage issues. I had to do a lot of work at home and at the family shop/bar.

Now that I'm a parent I can fully see and appreciate why my grandmother gave me these various tasks. The experience of learning through doing–the skills (in using the hands and articulating), discipline and responsibility I gained in Jamaica–have made me the woman I am today, even though at the time I thought my grandmother was a 'wicked woman' to be giving me so much to do.

If you grew up with a disciplinarian you know what I am talking about. Now that I am a mother and a wife, I thank her every day for what she's taught me.

It wasn't until I returned to the UK in 2000 and saw many women my age lacking in the things my grandmother taught me that I realised what a blessing it was to have grown up with them in rural Jamaica. Throughout my years in Jamaica, I carried a personal loneliness that went undetected by anyone who knew me. I was (and still am) a bubbly, happy-go-lucky person, always cracking a joke, but inside was a different story. I used to write letter after letter to my dad even though I knew he wouldn't see or read them, and often I'd lock myself in a room and spoke to myself, going through conversations with either my mother or father.

I went through many ups and downs growing up in Jamaica, but one important thing in life–I'd like to stress this to parents–is to ensure your children are able to approach and speak to you openly about anything.

Don't be too much of a righteous parent. Let them feel able to share their thoughts and opinions with you, as this will shed some light on what is going through their minds and will put you in a position to discuss any misunderstandings or wrong opinions they may have. This is exactly what happened to me. I chose to confide and seek solace in the wrong places with the wrong people at times. However, I was doing brilliantly in school and devoted in church– the only place I was allowed to go. I attended the Salvation Army and enjoyed it because of the numerous youth activities that I got involved with, as well as the loads of church trips I was able to go on.

I was a well-behaved young lady, church-goer, one of the highest achievers in my class at school, a member of the school debate team, a student councillor and a class prefect. This, however, did not stop me from going down the wrong path as I sought companionship in a boyfriend.

I completed Frome Technical High School in 1998 on a high note: For the first time, our school debate team, which included me and three other classmates, won the Credit Union Westmoreland Annual Debate competition. I was a 'bookworm'; wherever you saw me, I had a book, as I loved reading and would drown my sorrows either by reading or writing down my thoughts.

I got pregnant in 2000 and returned to the UK in December, where I gave birth to my beautiful daughter Santana in March 2001. I met my son's dad in 2002 and he brought out the worst in me. Once he went into a jealous rage and hit me in the head with a TV remote. I had never been so full of fury, I thought: *Right, I've had enough!* Enraged, I ran outside, found a brick, aimed it at our car and smashed one of the headlights. Stupidity, I call it now. I say 'our' car, he was the driver but it was my money that bought the car. And can you believe he called the police on me? They questioned me and I told them everything except that he had hit me.

They didn't lock me up, but told me to come with them to cool down; they talked with me whilst I was there. That is when a female police officer informed me it was him who had called them telling them he looked through the window and saw a mad woman smashing his car and he was scared to come out and confront her. I have to smile when I look back at where I have come from to where I am now.

Although I've not mentioned a fraction of things he has done, preferring to leave things at what the children already know, I learned to forgive him, and that was my greatest challenge. In spite of many threatening and abusive phone calls, I still said to him, 'God bless you'. The hatred I felt started to make me bitter to the point where I was living miserably. I remember hearing a woman in church quote a statement made by the great Nelson Mandela: 'Un-forgiveness is you drinking poison and expecting your enemy to die'. Truly this was the case, because every time I remembered all he'd done, my blood started to boil. I realised that in order for me to move on in true happiness I had to let go, let someone else do the hating, not me.

I can never forget the day I received a text from him asking for forgiveness and hoping I could find it in my heart to forgive him for all he'd done to me. I smiled–not out of pride, but because I had given my life to the Lord and already received the grace to forgive him. I was content, happy and no longer dwelled on the past. He had no choice to give up his hated fight, because he was no longer getting the reaction he expected from me.

I strongly believe I had to go through what I did to enable the glory of God to shine through. My husband now is a source of strength, and if I had not let go of my ex-husband, I would not have been with my husband now but instead would have held on to the experience I had with the fear it would repeat itself. Many of you do this especially in the areas of business or relationships, because you tried and failed before, you now let opportunities pass by because you are scared of failing again. Quite rightly, many of you may say that it's your beginning that matters and makes you who you are, which in some cases I agree with. However, Chris Gardner once said at a seminar I attended that you should not use a bad start as an excuse to have a bad end. You can correct your journey even if you got lost along the way; you may not be able to turn back the clock, but you can determine what you will do with the rest of your time.

> *You should not use a bad start as an excuse to have a bad end*

* * *

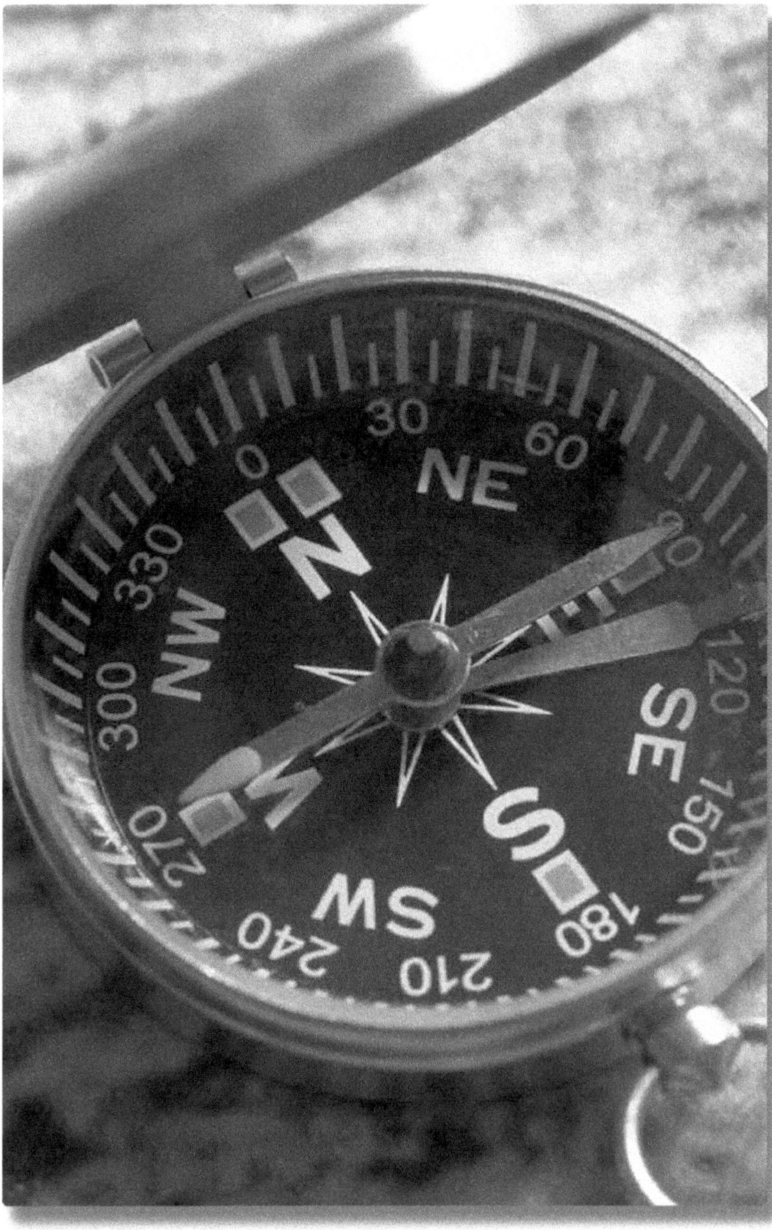
0
30
60
NE
N
330
NW
300
120
SE
150
S
180
210
SW
240
270
W

3
Get Rid of Fear

"Fear is a darkroom where negatives develop."
— Usman B. Asif

* * *

My son is a very loving boy, helpful and full of life. On meeting him for the first time, one would look at his innocent little face and immediately fall in love with him. However, impressions gradually change, when you see the other side of him.

Rashaun started Devonshire Hill Reception in Tottenham North London at the age of three and was loved by his teacher straight away, but as time went on complaints began to pour in on a daily basis: 'Your son hurt another child; he had a major temper tantrum and threw all the toys on the floor'. I used to feel so stressed out picking him up from school. It was absolutely horrible having other parents stare and look at me while the teacher reeled off the list of the day's ordeals. At this point, fear crept into my life; negativity hovered over every thought, because that is what fear does–it cripples all your dreams, positivity, confidence and hopes.

I came to realise that I had developed a fear of taking Rashaun anywhere. I always expected something bad to happen, and it would invariably happen just as I expected.

What, then, is fear? The Oxford Dictionary of English has four definitions of the noun fear: (1) An unpleasant emotion caused by the threat of danger, pain or harm; (2) a feeling of anxiety concerning the outcome of something or the safety of someone; (3) the likelihood of something unwelcome happening; and (4) a mixed feeling of dread and reverence (e.g., the love and fear of God). Wikipedia gives the definition of fear as 'an emotion induced by a perceived threat which causes entities to quickly pull away from it and usually hide'. My testament has elements of all these definitions. Many of you will be familiar with this popular acronym for fear: False (F) evidence (E) appearing (A) real (R). A church brother of mine told me another possible acronym for fear: Forgetting (F) everything (E) and (A) and run (R), meaning that you forget all the encouragement, direction and words of wisdom; you forget that God is a miracle worker who never fails, despite our circumstances. We forget all of this, holding on to that feeling of failure, disappointment and negativity. Then we run with these. I have done this so many times, so you are not on your own.

Things reached a point that sometimes I am somewhere with my son and I see another child crying and walking over to their parents and I start to panic, thinking that Rashaun has done something wrong. Fear tended to set in before I took the opportunity to find out what had really happened. Fear blinded me from seeing my son's good qualities or discovering the truth of who he could really be–making me constantly focus on false evidence instead of the possibility that just maybe Rashaun had not done anything wrong.

If it's possible that you can start a successful business, maybe it is worth taking the risk. Many people allow fear to drive them to fail before they have even tried. The very moment you think of one positive, your mind has allowed twice as much fear to pop up as to why you should not make the step. Fear is designed for you to find excuses to fail. It is up to you to amend your mindset and overcome it by doing the opposite, leave all the negatives behind, which also includes the negative people who are always telling you that you can't.

I soon came to the realisation I was attracting to myself the things that I expected; fear blinds you from seeing any light at the end of the tunnel. When people came to me and said, 'don't worry, he'll change', just like clockwork, fear began to remind me of the past, clouding my thoughts and dreams about my son's future. I used to reply sarcastically by saying, 'yeah, right'. I soon realised that fear came in the moment I didn't believe that God was able to change the unchangeable and turn around the impossible to the possible.

Many parents go through fear of their children getting hurt, being raped, kidnapped, killed, marrying or partnering with the wrong person, or making poor choices that will largely determine the quality of their future, among other worries. When those bouts of fear used to arrive, my stomach would do somersaults and I felt sick at the thought of something unwelcome happening to my children, as I would have done my all to prevent it. But how much can you protect your children? We have to allow them to be cut from our apron strings at some point; this, I must admit, is not easy.

I remember the first time I decided to let Santana walk to and from school on her own, and fear brought to me every wrong thought imaginable, but if I had obeyed these thoughts, she would have never gained her own strength of responsibility and I would not have been able to work or live my own life. I would have allowed fear to control our life. I thank God that when it was time for Rashaun to go on his school's yearly trip to Pendarren in Wales, I had by then overcome that type of fear, by the grace of God, or else he would never have attended: I would have been too worried about what might go wrong. That mindset would have hindered his chances, just as many of you are probably allowing fear to hinder your chances of success. Of course, parents have no choice but to be concerned about possible dangers in the world. But what I have come to realise, from my own experience and from many years reading and reasoning, is that fear comes on us at the moment we don't believe that God is able to help.

Anytime fear speaks, let your belief in yourself speak louder.

* * *

I always think of the Biblical story of Matthew Chapter 8, when Jesus walks on the water. Once Peter realised it was Jesus, he asked to walk with Him on the water. Jesus said, 'Come', and Peter didn't hesitate. Everyone knows that regardless of the condition of the water, calm as glass or boisterous as a dragon, walking on any water is beyond natural human capabilities. However, faith is governed by supernatural laws, which we must remember when circumstances, tests and trials come our way. When natural law says, 'It is hopeless', and there seems no way out, with faith we can walk on the water (tests and trials) because we have the Word of God to stand on, just like Peter. It wasn't the water that held Peter up: It was the Word of God, and that word was 'come'. Peter was doing great until his attention was drawn to the waves, and fear gripped him. Satan came with fear and Peter let go of his faith. Anytime fear speaks, let your belief in yourself speak louder.

A train has different carriages and is connected together by something called a coupler. At both ends there are the leading cars, which determine the speed, direction and destination of the other carriages. Right at this moment, some of you reading may have allowed fear to be the leading car in your lives, dictating what you can and can't do, which in the end determines your direction and destination.

Fear is not beneficial to us at all. Bible verse 2 Timothy 1:7 states, 'For God has not given us a spirit of fear, but of power and of love and of a sound mind'. A spirit of fearfulness and timidity does not come from God. However, sometimes this 'spirit of fear' overcomes us, and to overcome it we need to trust in and love God completely. For example, Isaiah 41:10 encourages us, 'Do not fear, for I am with you; Do not anxiously look about you, for I am your God. I will strengthen you, surely I will help you. Surely I will uphold you with my righteous right hand'.

Often we fear the future and what will become of us and our children. Sometimes some fear can be good; when you are afraid things are going to get worse if you don't do something, it can push you into action. An example of this was when my daughter Santana at the age of twelve asked me if I had made a will. It scared me a little, as I then thought what would happen if I died; what would be left behind for my children? You must balance fear's negative effects with its good ones. For instance, once I was so afraid I did not want to go and pick my son up from school. I had to develop the fear in me that drove me to help my son change his future as opposed to fearing what he might become. We begin to worry of what lies ahead that we begin to imagine all kinds of frightening stuff that could happen; so you have to learn how to let go and start trusting God. It is not easy but I had to tell myself that if I don't help him, who will? And with that the right fear came, the one that pushed me into an action mama.

In Psalm 56:11, the psalmist writes, 'In God I trust; I will not be afraid. What can man do to me?' This is a great testimony to the power of trusting in God. Regardless of what happens, I will trust in God because I know and understand the power of God. The key to overcoming fear, then, is to renew your mindset totally, put complete trust in God and believe in yourself and who he created you to be. Trusting God is a refusal to give in to fear. This trust comes from knowing God and knowing that He is good. This has helped me a lot and has given the peace of mind to know that no matter how things go wrong, there is hope. I started believing in faith instead of fear. I began taking my son places with me in faith instead of fear, believing that he would be good instead of awaiting something bad to happen. I no longer had fear about picking him up from school but instead trusted God for good report. Many times the situation that arises is what we bring to reality through our fears. We tend to allow fear to hold us captive, but once you get past the fear, you will realise that you get to enjoy your success more than you could ever believe.

Begin seeing your life in a positive way and stop thinking about what you are losing. Stop dwelling on the negative of what is happening; instead, think about what you can actually gain from making the effort to take the bold step and make things happen. My pastor of many years taught about the topics of faith and fear in Bible study, which opened my eyes. One of the main things I learnt from Bible study is that circumstances come and go, so every time an issue came along, I told myself it will not be forever.

The Bible tells us that *if you have faith as small as a mustard seed, you can say to the mountain move, and it will move*. I used to think this Bible verse was written as a made-up story and was only applicable to Biblical times. I read it as a literal moving of a mountain, which as far as I was concerned is not possible. I grew to understand that the mountain mentioned in this verse is symbolic of the difficulties and impossible situations I was facing, and once I applied faith and believed then I could remove those mountains of debt, failure, abuse, ADHD-everything that seemed so hard in my life.

We all know the energy that is needed to climb a mountain. I told myself that I might not be able to physically move a mountain, but that I could climb over it. I decided to think of all that strength and perseverance I would have to use to climb Mount Everest and channelled it into being the mum my children needed–one who would do all it takes to make them have a successful future and PUSH (Pray and Persevere Until Something Happens). Fear will not allow you to have the victory you desire; it will only lie to you and tell you that it is not possible. I sometimes wonder where my son would be now if I had allowed fear to dominate. I would not have fought so hard to ensure that he overcame all the negative outcomes that I was told to expect for him. For instance, I was told not to expect too much of him academically; fear said to me, 'Oh no my son is going to be illiterate'. When I used to help him to read at nights, fear confirmed all the symptoms and signs I was told about regarding Rashaun's illness. It was not until I had faith that I was able to say, 'I am not accepting this for my son, and I'm taking action'.

I went to all the meetings and parenting classes for children with special education needs and got Rashaun a tutor. As soon as that happened, the situation improved immensely. Within the first two sessions, the tutor was able to pinpoint Rashaun's weaknesses and strengths, as he had experience working with children like Rashaun. The tutor told me, 'This boy is brilliant; he just needs someone with the patience to work with him'. He took him on. I am forever grateful to this tutor who had strong belief in Rashaun and never used his illness as an excuse; instead, he pushed him even more than the others because he genuinely believed in him. Rashaun went from a low achiever to one of the highest-level students, especially in mathematics. He went from a child who had never received a certificate to one who receives certificates constantly. One evening, the principal, Ms. D'Abrieu, said to me that Rashaun was one of their success stories–this coming from a school that I believe at one stage would have given anything to get rid of Rashaun because of his disastrous behaviour! Imagine if I had given up; do you want to be someone that ends up regretting you did not have faith to see possibilities instead of impossibilities?

LIKE MY FACEBOOK PAGE AND GET INSTANT UPDATES ON MY BOOK AS WELL AS FREE MOTIVATIONAL TIPS ON HOW TO OVERCOME YOUR CHALLENGES.
WWW.TINYURL.COM/BREAKFREE-CONSULTANCY

4
Forget the Disappointments and Shame

*"Shame corrodes the very part of us that
believes we are capable of change."*

— Brené Brown

* * *

According to the Oxford Dictionary of English, 'disappointment' is a mass noun meaning 'sadness or displeasure caused by the non-fulfilment of one's hopes or expectations'. The mass noun 'shame' means 'consciousness of wrong or foolish behaviour; loss of respect or esteem, dishonour'.

Disappointment differs from regret in that a person feeling regret focuses primarily on the personal choices that contributed to a poor outcome, while a person feeling disappointment focuses on the outcome itself.

Many people are disappointed in their children or themselves when reality does not meet their expectations. Shame, on the other hand, is a destructive message; it says you are flawed and who you are is not enough. Shamed is how I used to feel when I saw my son being reprimanded by someone for doing something really embarrassing. As a parent in such situations, you question yourself for hours on end: 'Where have I gone wrong? What am I not doing right?' It makes you focus more on the problem than on the solutions. You enter into self-blame and, if not careful, you'll start feeling guilty.

In their enlightening book, *Facing Shame*, authors Fossum and Mason say, *'While guilt is a painful feeling of regret and responsibility for one's actions, shame is a painful feeling about oneself as a person'*. I now realise that my son felt the shame I felt at times, but I spent all my time thinking about how I was feeling instead of how he was feeling. Let me share a few situations with you to give you an idea of these circumstances. Envision yourself as a parent in these situations and imagine how you would feel. Once we went on a family and friends trip to Great Yarmouth. Everyone was having a good time, including all the kids, who were playing and running about.

A little boy of about the age ten left his drink where Rashaun was and went to the toilet. Rashaun urinated in the boy's drink, gave it a good shake then put it back down for the boy to drink it. Luckily and thankfully, when the boy returned, Rashaun and the other children who knew what he'd done were laughing; the boy picked up the bottle to drink and realised something was wrong and didn't drink it. When Rashaun's action came out, the little boy complained to his parents.

They were absolutely furious, and who could blame them? I would have been the same if that had happened to my child. Now, imagine yourself as a parent being in this situation. The shame and disappointment you would feel would drive you to question your parenting skills and yourself.

Another incident took place once when we went to my aunt's house for a family dinner. When we returned home, I noticed something bulging from Rashaun's left pants pocket, which prompted my husband to search him. He had taken my cousin's expensive watch, which clearly he didn't need; it was a female watch and he was just nine years old. What was his purpose in taking it? What did the object and the action mean to him? I called my aunt and made her aware of what had happened, returned the watch and everything was sorted. My cousin understood and forgave him for taking her watch, but for a long time that didn't remove the feeling of shame and disappointment I felt. Since this incident, we've developed the habit of searching Rashaun on returning home from visits. Oh, the shame of knowing that we felt it necessary to search our nine-year- old son on every occasion he returns home from visiting somewhere.

To make things worse, we visited that aunt's house again and after she left, she was not able to find her phone for weeks. Due to the previous incident with the watch, Rashaun was automatically the main suspect. However, I questioned him and he denied it and for some reason, I believed him. Possibly a motherly instinct, but I believed him. Unfortunately, though, the longer the phone couldn't be found, the more he was interrogated. I remember going to the bathroom one morning and praying earnestly, asking God to reveal what happened to the phone. I asked God that, if Rashaun took it, to let us find out so that we could address the issue; or if it was in the house or stolen by someone else, to let it be recovered so it would no longer hang over Rashaun's head. One night, weeks later, my aunty was looking for her passport because she was going to travel–and she found her phone! Can you imagine? The shame of my son being suspected for the missing phone now affected us all. Because of his previous actions, Rashaun had allowed himself to become a suspect too often and too easily. This has had a crushing impact on us as parents.

Such behaviour also impacts those who at first appear to be victim; like my aunt. When her phone was eventually found my aunt also experienced shame, due to the fact that she had already come to the wrong conclusion that Rashaun had taken it.

There are many instances of embarrassment caused by my son's outbursts of anger, often at various social events. The incident that affected me the most happened the day before his tenth birthday. It was a Sunday afternoon, and we had come from church and finished having dinner. Rashaun asked us if he could join the children playing outside. We agreed, especially because his behaviour that day was so outstanding, for which he was rewarded extra pocket money. He was out for about an hour before he asked if he could play computer games with our neighbour's son, which he had done before. When it was time for him to come in and get ready for bed, before I went to get him from my neighbour, he knocked on the door.

Upon entering he rushed upstairs, saying he was going to have his bath. I was very impressed and remarked to his step dad that he was really making an effort. Approximately five minutes later, there was a knock on my door. When I opened the door, there was a group of children with adults and onlookers outside.

I noticed a little boy crying and a woman beside him (whom later I learned was his mother) and asked what was wrong.

The mother was hysterical, speaking very franticly in a different language. A younger lady stepped forward to translate, and explained the dilemma to me. After Rashaun had finished next door, instead of coming home he went across the road to play with some other children. He took a four-year-old boy to a park about five minutes' walk from our house without anyone knowing. The mother of the boy eventually noticed he was missing, raised an alarm and started a search for him. She was just about to call the police when some older kids found them. Rashaun had made the little boy strip off his clothes in the park and repeatedly hit him with a stick until the boy was covered with bruises. I was speechless. Tears ran down my cheeks and I went into a mode of numbness when I realised that my son was capable of doing what these people were saying to me about him.

After many apologies from me and deliberations, the lady decided not to call the police. She said that at first she had believed that a child who does something like this could only come from a home of hooligans, but that on meeting us she realised we were nothing of the sort.

I couldn't sleep that night; the little boy and his mother were on my mind. Neither could I bring myself to speak to Rashaun about the incident, as I had no idea what to say to him or what punishment to give. I felt so ashamed and disappointed I had to pray and ask God to guide me; I kept thinking to myself, how could I go outside and face these people? I got up the following morning, which was Rashaun's birthday, knowing exactly what I was going to do, or more to the point, what I had to do. I needed to ensure that such an incident would never be repeated. We had bought Rashaun the latest Play Station Portable Console (the PS Vita) for his birthday. We showed this to him and then I told my husband to take it back to the shop where we bought it. I then told Rashaun to pack the Play Station and games he already had and accompany me to the little boy's house. When we got there I asked the mother about him and was shocked when she informed me that he was scared to go outside. My heart sank. I told Rashaun to apologise to the lady and hand her the bag with the console and games. At first she didn't want to take it, saying that they were kids and Rashaun's apology was enough.

I insisted, explaining that Rashaun needed to realise the seriousness of what he had done and how he affected her son. I hoped that losing something that meant more to him than anything else would ensure he never did it again. I expect some may think I was a bit harsh, but can you imagine being in such a disappointing situation? All that kept going through my head was I needed to ensure I did the right thing. Just as I did not want my children to be victims of anyone else's crime, I didn't want them to be criminals or anyone be victims of their wrongdoing. There's no benefit to having your child playing on expensive games if he has no morals. After Rashaun handed over the bag, he stormed off in anger, hurling abuse at me, telling me how he hated me–this was on the street, with people hearing and looking. I could only imagine what they must have been saying.

I had a long talk with Rashaun and asked him why he did what he did. He said that he had seen it on the TV and thought it was fun. I made him understand why I did what I did, but most of all I made him know that I still love him. Never assume your child knows that you still love them after they have done wrong.

Tell and show them in ways they understand that in spite of everything, you still love them. After speaking with Rashaun that night, I hugged him and told him that I loved him and would not give up on him, because I knew he was a good boy destined for greatness. But it was a long time before I sent Rashaun outside to play with the kids in the neighbourhood again, because I expected that that specific incident wouldn't vanish from other parents' memories: I knew they would be very wary about allowing their children to play with Rashaun again.

There were, however, times when Rashaun got blamed for things he didn't do because he had become an easy target for other children to point fingers at. There were times when Rashaun was not even involved, but got blamed anyway; how frustrating such times were for both of us. It was just so unfair for him. Even at home, if anything went wrong, Rashaun would be under fire straight away. When it came to his behaviour, no one took the time to investigate anything. It was a lot easier to blame Rashaun first and then investigate later.

If I were to detail all the incidents my son has been involved in that have brought disappointment or shame on my family, this testament would never end. Some of you hearing me attempt to encourage parents with children experiencing similar difficulties as my son may think, 'Oh, she doesn't know what she's talking about' or 'She has no idea what I am going through'. However, even if the individual child will behave in a specific way in a given situation, I know the feeling of shame and disappointment that behaviour brings and how to overcome it. It does take a long time to be resilient when handling disappointment and shame, for individuals who have tried their hands at achieving anything, whether it is a business venture, financial freedom or a relationship.

Remember that our own approach, expectations and circumstances have a great part to play when dealing with difficult challenges, so we have to work continuously to understand how we react in certain situations and how we express emotions such as fear and anger, etc. As you grapple with all of this, you will learn from your experience, so when the feeling of disappointment or shame comes, do not give up.

You cannot choose to remain in the comfort zone because it suits you or because someone has said that's where you should or only have the capacity to be; as the great Les Brown always says *'Someone's opinion of you does not have to become your reality'*.

Being successful is not about showing your strength in your strong areas but being able to show strength in the areas where you would have the tendency to be weak. You can choose to remain disappointed and ashamed or become motivated to learn from your mistakes, brush yourself off when you fall, and ensure that you don't allow history to repeat itself. Do not dwell or focus on your own disappointment and shame. Spend your time finding ways of helping yourself or, if you are a parent, help your child; doing so will produce the best results and will prevent disappointment and shame from turning to resentment towards yourself or your child.

5
What is your Diagnosis?

Diagnosis is not the end, but the beginning of practise.
— Martin H. Fischer

* * *

I've spent countless hours running from one meeting to another. It reached a point where, just to keep my son in school, he had to be assessed to see if there were any underlying issues and so that the school would be able to get the assistance needed from the government. Our first application to the Special Education Needs Panel was turned down, but we persisted until we were directed to the Child and Adolescent Mental Health Services (CAMHS), who needed to assess him themselves. This involved more meetings in addition to what I already had to cope with. By this time, I understood what's meant by the term 'headless chicken', but I kept telling myself, 'Don't give up, Michelle; you have to fight for your son'. We eventually had the assessment by CAMHS, but as usual, there were complications: CAMHS had to carry out further assessments, as there were signs of both autism and attention deficit hyperactivity disorder (ADHD). After more assessments, they finalised his diagnosis as ADHD.

What is ADHD?

Attention deficit hyperactivity disorder is another stage of attention deficit disorder (ADD). The former is characterised by inattention plus impulsiveness, whereas a child with ADHD suffers from inattention, impulsiveness and hyperactivity.

ADHD is one of the most common childhood disorders and can continue through adolescence and adulthood. Symptoms include difficulty staying focused and paying attention, difficulty controlling behaviour and hyperactivity (over-activity). It is normal for all children to have phases of inattentiveness, hyperactivity or impulsivity, but for children afflicted with ADHD, these behaviour patterns are more severe and occur more often. For a child to be diagnosed with the disorder, for six or more months he/she must show symptoms that are greater in degree than those found in other children of the same age. Although the symptoms of ADHD can be nothing short of exasperating, it's important to remember that the child troubled with ADHD is not acting wilfully whenever he/she ignores, annoys or embarrasses you. The exact cause of ADHD is not fully understood, but a combination of factors is thought to be responsible.

Some of these factors include genetics; brain function and structure (people with ADHD have a number of brain differences from those who don't have the condition); premature birth or low birth weight; brain damage (either in the womb or in the first few years of life); prenatal exposure to alcohol, nicotine or drugs, amongst other things. However, the evidence is inconclusive regarding the impact of these respective factors.

Diet plays a major part in your child's progress and behaviour, which Dr. Sally Bundae, MBE, founder of the Hyperactive Children's Support Group (HCSG) emphasised in an interview. Dr. Bundae emphasised that a healthy diet is a major factor in the progress of a child diagnosed with hyperactivity syndrome; however, many do not pay careful attention to this factor and only focus on medication as a cure, instead of also acknowledging the importance of a healthy diet.

You need to be honest with yourself and diagnose what it is that has caused the challenge you are going through right now, so that you know the correct steps to take.

* * *

Rashaun's diagnosis was able to help us recognise his needs and entitled him to receive a statement of Special Education Needs, which is a legal document laying out the details of special needs your child is considered to have. The statement outlines the specific help that your child has a right to and that will be made available to meet your child's needs. It enabled Rashaun and the school to receive funding, which provided additional resources. It does not eradicate all the issues but provides a source of support. Whatever your challenge, don't run away from it but face it head on by investigating and finding out as much as you can in order to understand how to address it. If you don't know anything about your challenge and avoid it, you will never overcome or rise above it.

You need to be honest with yourself and diagnose what it is that has caused the challenge you are going through right now, so that you know the correct steps to take.

Eventually, I came to the realisation that my son really wanted to sit quietly, make his room tidy and organised and do everything he was told to do, but he didn't know how to make these things happen. While going through the CAMHS tests, I had to complete a lengthy checklist of the signs and symptoms I associate with my son. I ticked off some of the following:

- Is easily distracted, misses details, forgets things and frequently switches from one activity to another.
- Difficulty focusing attention on organising and completing a task or learning something new.
- Often loses things (e.g., pencils, toys, assignments).
- Doesn't seem to listen when spoken to.
- Struggles to follow instructions.
- Fidgets and squirms.
- Talks nonstop and dashes around, touching or playing with anything and everything in sight.
- Is constantly in motion.
- Blurts out inappropriate comments, shows their emotions without restraint, and acts without regard for consequences.
- Has difficulty waiting for things they want or their turn in games.
- Is disorganised and easily distracted.
- Has impulsivity issues that often interrupt conversations.
- Has difficulty getting to bed and to sleep.
- Is hyperactive and has no fear of danger.
- Is totally oblivious to the effect their actions have on others and may find it funny when others get hurt.

Imagine the impact this had on me and my household. There was my husband, who at the time must have been asking himself what he had got himself into; there were Santana and Alisha, who Rashaun wasted no time in aggravating along the way. At the time Rashaun was diagnosed with ADHD, Alisha was not yet born, but since her birth the impact of his behaviour has been no less on her than it has been on his elder sister. Coping with children diagnosed with ADHD affects parents in many ways. The demands are as physically draining (and that is putting it lightly), as the need to monitor activities, meetings and actions are psychologically exhausting. The child's inability to listen or behave, and your knowledge of the consequences, is numbing. This makes you anxious and stressed, causing you to expect the worse to happen, which limits you and your child. You'll want to stop going places or joining activities because of that fear that things will go wrong. All of this frustration can lead to anger, the ultimate crusher of any vision or hope that you may have not just for you, but for the whole family, as everyone feels the impact. I felt like Xena the warrior princess, constantly overcoming different enemies and, eventually, being victorious in battles.

It has been difficult to keep everyone happy and everything in order. My husband, for instance, at times felt that the challenge was all too much for him. Who could blame him? At first when he came to live with us, he was able to cope, but over a period of time the challenges became draining, especially because the frequency of issues escalated as Rashaun grew older. One issue was we were constantly interrupted by the school requesting we leave work to come and get Rashaun immediately. Any marriage or family that has to deal with challenging children will face issues that are specific to them. However, if you work together and have good communication with each other, you will be able to address these challenges more effectively.

You would be surprised at the number of families that have been broken due to this lack of communication. What helped my family most was praying and making God our foundation. The Book of Psalms became an important read in my family. Chapter 127:1 tells us that, 'Except the Lord builds the house they labour in vain who build it…' This chapter became a mainstay for my family and me through the years, as we kept telling ourselves that without God as our foundation, we would not have the strength to overcome.

The passage also brightened up those mornings that seemed as if they were going to be the worst and warmed up some of the coldest nights we had experienced. I am sure at times my husband must have felt like strangling me, because I felt like doing the same to him at times too. Half of the time we didn't know if we were coming or going. This exhausting to and fro put an enormous strain on our social life, which was now reduced to eating, working, going to meetings, and sleeping.

At times we would end up losing patience with ourselves and the children. Remember the saying: 'All work and no play make Jack a dull boy'. The same applies to a marriage. After my husband and I had been on this rollercoaster for a while, I could see dullness creeping into our marriage. We made a decision to nip it in the bud at a very early stage by starting to take more time out for ourselves, the other children and making time for all of us together in order to keep the joy and happiness alive in our household.

Although constant prayer, good communication and bonding within the family will help keep joy and happiness in the household, it's easy to see that the symptoms of ADHD affect everyone, especially siblings. I realised that my girls faced a number of challenges because of Rashaun's condition:

- Their needs often got less attention than those of the child with ADD/ADHD.
- They were rebuked more sharply when they erred, and their successes were less celebrated or taken for granted.
- Santana was often enlisted as an assistant parent–and blamed if Rashaun misbehaved under her supervision.
- As a result, they found their love for Rashaun mixed with jealousy and resentment.

At times I felt not only like Xena the warrior princess, but also like a referee between my children. I know most of you with more than one child have an idea of how it feels, but now imagine that feeling multiplied by two. It was a lot more than just the physical fight. It became emotionally draining, trying to keep peace between everyone in the house as resentment started to rear its ugly head.

6
Let Go of Resentment and Hurt

"Tose who really love you don't mean to hurt you and if they do, you can't see it in their eyes but it hurts them too."

— Holly Black

* * *

After a while, Santana developed resentment towards her brother and accused me of not paying attention to her, which as you can imagine, was painful to hear. All this came due to the amount of time and energy spent on the numerous meetings that I had to be involved with because of Rashaun. I tried my best to get her involved too, but all she could see was the attention I was giving to Rashaun. My husband and I had to take so much time off work to accommodate the various meetings and emergency call-out for us to come and remove Rashaun from school; it appeared that Rashaun's case had taken over our life, so it became almost impossible to take time off for something concerning Santana.

To help reduce her resentment and bridge the gap between her and her brother, I explained to her that the time spent focusing on Rashaun was necessary because of his medical condition, not because he is special or was my favourite as she believed; the worst thing was that I couldn't blame her for feeling this way.

My husband and I tried all we could to balance our time between them both and things went reasonably well until Alisha came–which made things even more difficult to handle!

At first Santana was not at all interested in Alisha, whilst Rashaun, on the other hand, was absolutely over the moon. I remember when I was pregnant he used to come into my room at nights and speak to my big belly, kiss it and say goodnight. So Alisha's arrival was a bitter-sweet experience. There was also an incident that happened between Santana and Rashaun for which she never seemed to forgive him. I was at work one day (whilst I was still married to Rashaun's dad) and received a call informing me that Rashaun had set Santana's head on fire. Rashaun was only two years old at the time, and Santana was four; both children were at home with my ex-husband and they were upstairs in the bedroom watching the television when a visitor knocked on the door. My ex-husband left his cigarette lighter on the bed and went to answer the door, not thinking that either of the children would be able to light it. While he was talking, he heard a loud scream; Rashaun had ignited the lighter and set Santana's hair on fire.

The fire was put out before it reached her scalp, although a good amount of her hair had burnt and she was left with a bald patch, and there was now a significant difference between the long, curly hair she had. I came home very grateful to God that the situation had not been any worse. I was still very upset and frightened because it could easily have been another story. However, in spite of the fact Rashaun was young at the time and we repeatedly explained to Santana he was unaware of the seriousness of his actions, she still did not let go of it, even when re-growth of her hair was complete, which took a long time. Rashaun never remembered the incident, but anytime there was an argument between them, Santana brought up the topic again. The resentment between the children got worse; if it was difficult for us to handle Rashaun's weird and spontaneous behaviour, it was twice as difficult for Santana. She had to deal with the constant changes in her body and lack of the attention she desperately craved, all the while sharing a room with her brother who did almost everything that made her life miserable. Santana became so embarrassed by Rashaun's behaviour that she didn't want to go anywhere with him or be seen with him.

Many times when we went out he would end up doing something so bad that we would return home prematurely, and Santana would once again feel she was missing out. My husband and I would sometimes have to split ourselves into two, so to speak: One would remain at the event so that Santana could stay and have a little fun whilst the other returned home with Rashaun. I tried so much to make the children have a positive relationship that it became a pain in my heart thinking my children would grow up hating each other. I remember days when I felt like breaking down in tears because I was certain Rashaun didn't deliberately want to hurt anyone; he just couldn't help himself at times. Many of you will recall the saying 'Idle hands are the devil's workshop'. Well, this is another way of understanding Rashaun and was one of his greatest challenges: Once he became bored in the house, he would release his energies by ensuring that Santana had the worst time of her life, which to him was great fun. Little did he know how much this distressed, infuriated and pushed her to greater levels of anger and frustration. Santana didn't appreciate or understand Rashaun's issues; all she could see was the anger and hurt that he inflicted on her and the disruption he was causing to her life.

I remember her saying, 'Things used to be so much better when it was just me alone', and my eyes flooded with tears because I understood how she felt. I wanted her to understand Rashaun's situation and have patience, but how could she? Even we adults found it difficult to be patient and quell the rising feelings of hurt and resentment towards Rashaun, which at the time was immensely difficult to do. No one really wants to harbour resentment, but once it's developed it takes time to remove it from your system. This, I realised at one point, was another challenge for me to overcome. Take a look at some of the following words related to resentment:

Bitterness, bad feelings, irritation, displeasure, dissatisfaction, disgruntlement, discontentment, hard feelings, ill feelings, animosity and hatred. Wikipedia states that resentment can result from a variety of situations involving an actual or perceived wrongdoing from an individual and often are sparked by feelings of injustice or humiliation.

Reading this definition of resentment resonated with the emotions that flew around my household. Many of those who had to deal with Rashaun would never admit they felt resentment towards him, but the truth was betrayed by their body language and attitude. I used to feel greatly pained and hurt to know that my child was being resented because I knew in the depths of my heart that he was not an easy child to deal with, but nevertheless deserving of full professional attention.

All that you accomplish in life can be attributed to your state and quality of the mind.

* * *

I also felt like I failed my son and that I didn't know what to do to help him. As a mother, I could also see the hurt he was feeling when he was shut out. Once, Rashaun came home very unhappy. I asked him what was wrong and he told me one of his classmates was having a birthday party and all the children were invited except him; my heart just broke because I knew the reason why. There have been numerous occasions when he has had to be left out, or we went somewhere and he was ridiculed because of his behaviour. Have you ever felt so low because of your child's behaviour that you start imagining how much better your life would be if they were not around? How terrible is that?

Let go and move on!

* * *

I can never forget the day that thought came to me. I felt sick to my stomach. I broke down and cried out of control because I love my son so much, but I was allowing resentment to enter in.

I prayed to God, asking him to help me remain strong, to be a good mother, wife and woman.

It is a vicious cycle and, as I said earlier, not correcting it in its infancy can destroy not only relationships within your household, but also the relationship with others. It is the sort of feeling that workers sometimes have towards their boss, and when this happens the boss can never get the full potential from that staff. All that you accomplish in life can be attributed to your state and quality of the mind, so it is important to maintain a positive attitude no matter how hard the negatives try to intrude. Let me remind you, quite often the negative will seem the easier option, but in the long run the negative will cause dismay. At times resentment has caused many to not receive the promotion or growth they are qualified for and could have easily have, because instead of letting go the little thing which is now causing resentment, they allowed it to fester to the point of paying more attention to it than their capabilities and goals. Let go and move on!

7
Perseverance

"Perseverance is the hard work you do after you get tired of doing the hard work you already did."
— *Newt Gingrich*

"How you do anything is how you do everything."
— *T. Harv Eker*

* * *

Perseverance is a steady persistence in a course of action–trying again and again. It is the inner machine that keeps you going. I realised that I had to be committed in all I did to have success

and not give up, no matter the circumstances. There were times I felt like giving up. I felt drained and discouraged and thought it made no sense to continue fighting what seemed to be a losing battle. At this point, ask yourself: If you give up, who will fight? For those of you not facing lack of perseverance as a parent, maybe you are as a student, in your business, or as an individual trying to overcome a specific challenge. Sometimes it takes very little to bring you to the point of giving up when you are not seeing the result you expected. Many want to achieve what they want comfortably, but if you're not yet successful and you're too comfortable, you are not far from experiencing poverty.

Taking risks is not comfortable: If you were to ask the most successful people in the world how they reached success, they will talk about an uncomfortable time in their life. At times, something very minor has propelled me into a feeling of failure or despair. I was often thrown into this bubble when I hadn't taken the time to have a break, calm down and rejuvenate myself. If someone has too much pressure building up inside without release, the stress will eventually become so burdensome that it will drain their ability to keep going.

My pastor would encourage me by telling me that there was a reason for everything I faced as a parent. But I wasn't much interested in hearing that; I just wanted it to be over so I could live peacefully. But if I hadn't had all my experiences, what help would I have been able to write about? People listen with more interest when they recognise that you have journeyed the road they are now travelling on. When you have persevered and overcome, you can look back at every moment of your journey and draw strength in knowing you have succeeded because you never gave up. This is the same for any individual regardless of their specific challenges.

Don't compare yourself to others.

* * *

Perseverance is the spirit of determination that drives us toward our goals, that keeps us going despite mountains of challenges and failures, that gives us the confidence to be flexible and prepared to change plans when things aren't working. Parents whose children present challenging behaviour and whose children have disabilities must realise that they may need to work harder and longer because of their children's difficulties. The same is true for individuals in any challenging circumstances, who have to put more effort than those who already have what they want. Do not compare yourselves to others; each individual's difficulties are unique and require different approaches to and levels of perseverance. In track and field athletics, I notice that the hurdler who focuses on the hurdles (the obstacles) stumbles, but the athlete who focuses on the finishing line ahead (the target) always complete the race without tripping or falling, even if they don't finish first. So focus on the solution you want for the difficulties you are facing, even if your strategies initially seem ineffective. Always keep in mind that your race does not belong to the swift; it is yours to win only if you endure to the end. My own experience proves this point.

The following will help you to persevere through challenges:

1. Learn how to manage stress and make time for yourself.
2. Ensure that you set realistic goals and develop the mental capacity to reach them.
3. Don't get hung up on small incidents. This energy could be used on something more productive.
4. Have confidence in yourself.
5. Don't compare yourself to others; we all have different strengths and talents, and drawing comparisons will put unfair pressure on you.
6. Avoid expressing negative words or opinions, as this can cast doubts on the possibilities. Engage with positive people and listen to and attend motivational speakers' seminars.

7. Learn from your mistakes. Wisdom is gained by making mistakes and trying something different the next time.
8. Stay resilient at all times.
9. Have faith. Believe in a positive outcome despite what reality is showing you.
10. Most importantly, feed your spiritual life.

These will help you persevere and find the strength needed to accomplish your goals. Remember, winners never quit and quitters never win. Don't take the easy way out; what you don't fight for today you will have to fight for tomorrow

SCAN THE CODE TO RECEIVE A CHECKLIST OF MUST DO'S WHEN FACING DIFFICULT CHALLENGES.
WWW.TWITTER.COM/SUCCESSINACTION

8
Don't Be Proud – Seek Help

> *"The first question which the priest and the Levite asked was: 'If I stop to help this man, what will happen to me?' But... the Good Samaritan reversed the question: 'If I do not stop to help this man, what will happen to him?'"*
>
> — Martin Luther King, Jr.

* * *

Naturally, when I started dealing with the parental issues I was facing, I was a complete novice, unsure of what to do when complications arouse. Don't be surprised that no matter how many books you read, when the actual situations arise, all that 'book knowledge' tends to be forgotten. Even this book you are reading can only serve as a guide and provide general insights into what to do; you will function fully only when you've had your own hands-on experience.

I worried about everything, which doesn't help when dealing with the impulsive actions of a child with ADHD, nor with the consequences of those unpredictable actions. I repeatedly asked myself, 'What am I doing wrong? What areas can I improve?' But take my advice: Never pressure yourself even when you don't get it right the first time. Learning comes with experience. Without my short-falls and failures along the way, I wouldn't have been able to write this book.

I once heard this question: 'Without a test, where will your testimony come from?' I gathered strength from writing this book, knowing that my experience might assist others now travelling the same journey I did not so long ago. Most successful people turned the pain they've experienced into their passion, and I can testify that this is true. Consider this: What do you tend to think of more, your joy or your pain? If we are honest, in spite of the fact that we prefer the happy moments, subconsciously we tend to focus more on things that went wrong because we either want to correct or prevent them happening again. The desire to raise beautiful, respectful and successful children pushed me through all the pain I felt. That pain then became my passion because I vowed that I would never give up or stop helping others. It is that same passion that helped me to complete this book and be able to help someone who is now in the shoes I once wore. One of the first and most important steps is to accept that something is wrong–and what is usually wrong is your mindset.

Until you are willing to renew your mind, no matter how many books you read, seminars you attend or motivational speakers you listen to, you will remain the same. As the great T. Harv Eker says, until you check your blueprint and revisit the root of your tree that produces bad fruits, your result will remain the same. As proud human beings, we never want to admit we need help, but the earlier we do the better it will be for everyone concerned. Reluctance to admit you need help is comparable to someone who is suffering from an addiction: Unless they admit that they have a problem, no one can help them, and denial closes the door to them receiving help. Until and unless we open up to ask for the help we need, we will not receive it. This is where a lot of us often get it wrong. We lock from our minds the imperfections of our children or ourselves, which some parents believe is a form of love. But if you really love your child, then you want the best in life for him or her. A child will always be short of something, even if they become the richest person in the world, but without the right morals they will certainly wither away.

You have to be observant and non-indulgent. Do not hide, deny or invent excuses for any misgivings. This goes not only for your child but also for you as an individual. Be honest with yourself about where you are going wrong and ask for help. There is nothing wrong with asking for help! At first I did not want to see or hear the worst in or about my children, but when things began to go further downhill, I had to wake up and face reality in time so that I didn't lose my child.

Becoming open to help is not easy because it includes hearing the truth, about yourself or your children, that you may be doing something wrong–and no one wants to accept that. When Rashaun was diagnosed as having ADHD, I didn't want to accept this diagnosis from the doctor, but at the same time I knew I had to listen in order to help my son. I had to accept that there was something wrong in order for it to be fixed.

I started to do my own research in ADHD, which you need to do for yourself so that you can have a clear understanding of the symptoms, and available help and what to expect. The professionals sent me to numerous meetings. Some were helpful, and others were of no help whatsoever. Even though I couldn't see the sense in attending some of the meetings and the whole experience was exhausting, I kept going, because I realised every piece of information was helpful. Take note of all the information you can without over- burdening yourself, even if you think it's not important at the time.

An essential entry in your help directory is having the right environment and people around you. The quality of your environment will greatly impact your life and that of your children, especially for those who are experiencing challenging behaviour and other disabilities. The last thing you need is people around you who will constantly point out the negatives. These people, and the environment their attitude creates, will cloud your positive thoughts and make you doubt any hope of improvement.

Circumstances come and go.

* * *

'No man is an island and no man stands alone'. You will need people around you who recognise the good that is in you, the ones who will not see only the weaknesses but also the strengths. I am celebrate the day my pastors came into my life; even though I had my family teaching me the practical positives of life, I lacked spiritual positivity and needed help in this area. My pastors assisted me spiritually and taught me how to effectively use positivity even when things seemed as if they could never get any worse. I learnt how to speak to my children and let them know I was there for them at all times. Applying advice from my pastor, I was able to remain much calmer (though not all the time, of course!). I learnt lessons of self-control, but the main thing that my pastor taught me was that circumstances come and go. I realised that it's not the challenge but how you handle it that will determine the outcome. Minister Kudzi, the children's Sunday school teacher, was also a positive example, offering support, talking or giving advice to them when they felt they couldn't speak to me.

This support is very important, as sometimes children find it easier to speak to someone who is not their parent.

Don't be upset if this happens. It is a good thing, once you are confident that the person is a trustworthy confidant and positive influence. Don't allow your child to go looking for the wrong listening ear. My church was my home away from home, where I was able to find much needed peace of mind, sense of purpose and the encouragement to carry on. At church, I knew my children wouldn't be judged on the basis of their weaknesses. The practical, on-the-ground, everyday support of your family is also equally important for helping your child through his/her difficulties.

I enjoy the blessing of having both a close-knit biological family and spiritual family involved in the guidance of my children. My biological family is the rock on which I built my circle of support. My dad was always there for the little manly talks with Rashaun; my older cousin, Wayne, served as the disciplinarian when things got out of hand; other family members acted as listening ears. Some could be relied on to do emergency pickups from school and others took turns having the children for a few days so that we could have a break every now and then.

I thank God for providing me with such a helpful and supportive family that, no matter our issues, have the ability to overcome and move forward. Children should grow up knowing and valuing the importance of good family relationships.

My children's home tutor also made great impact on my children's lives For him, teaching is not about money but a way to fulfil his passion for educating children and ensuring that they perform to the best of their abilities. I remember the very first time he met Rashaun. After spending an hour with him, he said to me that Rashaun was a very talented young man who just needed the proper support. Indeed, Rashaun received this help from him. When they started working together, Rashaun could hardly read, write or do anything, and he had been written off when it came to academics. After working with the tutor for approximately six months, we could see big differences in Rashaun's school work.

I also cannot overstate the importance of building a close relationship with the school your child attends. The better the relationship you have with the school, the more effort will be made for your child. I must admit that Rashaun's school and I had a rocky start, but soon we realised we needed help from each other to make our respective plans work.

There is always help no matter what area it is needed, so go out and find it!

9
Live Solutions, Not Problems

"Every problem has in it the seeds of its own solution. If you don't have any problems, you don't get any seeds."

— Norman vincent Peale

* * *

There is no one solution when it comes to dealing with challenges; everything is trial and error until a solution is found. You can go down many avenues to figure out what works best for you, as we are all challenged in many different ways. Children diagnosed with ADD or ADHD generally have deficits in what is termed executive functions: The ability to think and plan ahead, organise, control impulses and complete tasks. That means parents need to take over as the executive role-player, thinking, planning and providing extra guidance while the child gradually acquires the skills of his or her own. Although coping with the symptoms can be nothing short of exasperating, it's important to remember that the child afflicted with these conditions, who is ignoring, annoying, or embarrassing you, is not acting purposely. Having the condition can be just as frustrating for the child as the parent.

If you keep this in mind, it will be a lot easier to respond to your child with patience, compassion, positivity and support. All children need to have love, encouragement and support; for those with learning disabilities, such positive reinforcement ensures that they emerge with a strong sense of self-worth, confidence and determination to keep going even when circumstances are tough. Many parents prefer having the friendship of the child, at the expense of implanting discipline. But a child develops self-worth through discipline and discipline through love, patience and trust.

I couldn't see any way forward when I kept focusing on the problems instead of finding the solutions; the reality instead of the possibilities. Many spend more time paying attention to the wrong things that hinder their growth, blinding them from seeing what would not only add value but also eliminate their problems, even as these worthwhile pursuits are staring them right in the face.

Every invention arose in order to provide a solution to a problem. There is no challenge that you can overcome by focusing on your suffering rather than the solution. Instead, pay attention to what you will need to eradicate your challenges. I love Andy Harrington's book titled *Passion into Profit–How to Make Big Money from Who You Are and What You Know*. Your experiences make you an expert in the challenge you overcame (Your Experience Ph.D.). If you can turn that pain from your challenge into a passion to spread knowledge, you can not only help others but make big money at the same time. I will never be afraid to make money using what I have learned through my challenging experiences. Someone might say, I thought you said you wanted to help others. My reply is a resounding YES– but how many can I reach and help if I am not earning money myself?

Don't agonise and grumble about the problem; instead, STOP and think SOLUTIONS.

Don't agonise and grumble about the problem; instead, STOP and think SOLUTIONS.

* * *

10
Hope, Positive Speaking and Mindset

"Hope is like the sun, which, as we journey toward it, casts the shadow of our burden behind us."

— Samuel Smiles

"Words can poison, words can heal. Words start and fight wars, but words make peace. Words lead men to the pinnacles of Good and words can plunge men to the depths of evil."

— Marguerite Schumann

* * *

What is hope? I commence with this question because some people often get confused or are unaware that hope is slightly different from having a desire or a wish.

The difference is that hope is a feeling of expectation of obtaining a particularly desired outcome; it is an aspiration, a dream, a yearning. Hope, then, is the mindset that looks forward, 'expecting with confidence'. Without hope, you will never stand a chance of winning the battle. Hope kept me going, and the belief one day things will become better gave me the endurance I needed to persevere even when I started to crumble. Hope revived and pushed me back into action. It is harder to achieve what you want if you allow yourself to become swayed by what's going on in the present. Hope, therefore, nourishes the belief you have in yourself. It's this belief that will encourage you to keep trying to achieve.

Hope gave Rashaun the desire for improvement and the belief that these goals were attainable. I kept that picture in my mind of what things could be, rather than what they are. By doing so, I was able to develop and maintain high hopes for Rashaun, my family and myself. Focus more on the positive and find alternatives instead of thinking negatively and feeling stifled by the 'nothing's gonna work' attitude. Replace negative thoughts with positive ones because fear will over-shadow the hope and possibility that the situation will work out. When hope is gone, you'll be tempted to give up.

Note that hopefulness is not blind optimism; it isn't putting on a smiling face in every situation. Obstacles and drawbacks are inevitable; you still have to expect that things will go wrong sometimes. But hope opens the door to having a positive belief in yourself, which you will need in order to overcome all the negatives you're likely to face in the world.

The mere glimmer of hope will keep you going until you have achieved your end result. It is very easy to lose hope, but having the right mindset will redirect you to your place of hope. Never let anyone fool you; whether it is a personal goal, family crisis or challenge with your children, hope makes a big difference to the task of finding solutions.

James MacNeil

Hope presented itself to me when I met James MacNeil at Success 2015 in ExCeL London. He is a successful businessman, speaker, motivator and author of the book titled *7e Guru Builder*, and he knew all too well what my son was going through, as he had walked the journey himself. He had even greater difficulty because he was not diagnosed until the age of 30 and received no help, despite displaying all the symptoms. He was just seen as a 'little brat', a ' jerk' and a problem child who just needed a few good slaps. All that he was crying out for was acceptance and not to be hated. However, by the age of 11, he was hated even more by adults and yearned for their acceptance.

James struggled with his speech and had to have speech therapy at age nine. Children with ADHD have a mind that operates with such speed that sometimes the mouth struggles to keep up. When I asked James how all of this made him feel, he replied, 'lonely and heartbroken'. This was painful to hear, as I thought about Rashaun and how he must be feeling. This great Guru Builder had overcome depression, homelessness, attempted suicide and even ventures into drug dealing; his loneliness and desire to fit in became so great that he hoped to be killed. This is when he realised he had gone wrong. He was trying so hard to fit in where he didn't, instead of discovering who he really was and where he did fit in.

When interviewing James, I asked him what turning point directed him onto a new path and led him to success. I was not surprised when he replied, 'God'. With the realisation that God loved him despite his faults and forgave him, he was able to forgive himself and commence his spiritual journey, which helped him find his way. He no longer lived to fit in but instead lived to honour God and fulfil his purpose.

James is now able to recognise his areas of weakness and strengths. He admits he is rubbish at paperwork and admin duties, but he no longer stresses about those weaknesses. Instead, he has positioned himself so that he is now able to hire others to handle those challenging errands. He can then focus on his own strengths: He can package and comprehend complex ideas, and what we would struggle with for hours he could resolve in a matter of minutes.

James's greatest strength is revealed where I first saw him–on stage, speaking and transforming lives. He realised that he was doing what most of us do, which is to focus so much on our failures that we hinder our own success. His advice to those diagnosed with ADHD is to find what calms your soul. For James it's driving or taking a walk. Most importantly, he talks about forgiving yourself, accepting who you are and managing your difficulties by finding your purpose. His past challenges enable him to be grateful for his progress and for the unique strength, knowledge and control he has acquired–the feeling of overcoming challenges through the grace of God.

Finally, I asked James whether he would have preferred an easier beginning, as so many of us desire. The obvious answer was 'Yes'. But he then referenced a dialogue from *The Lord of The Rings*:

> '*Frodo: I wish the Ring had never come to me. I wish none of this had happened.*
>
> *Gandalf: So do all who live to see such times, but that is not for them to decide. All we have to decide is what to do with the time that is given to us. There are other forces at work in this world, Frodo, besides the will of evil*'.

James then followed with his favourite quote by Oliver Wendell Holmes, which has provided him with insight on his journey:

> 'One of the greatest tragedies of our time is most
> people die with their music still in them'.

I watched James MacNeil, this Guru Builder, on stage. I admired the impact he had on the audience, how they hung on his every word, and the applause he received when he finished. I left the seminar floating, feeling a new sense of hope that Rashaun's challenges could be managed and overcome.

Positive Confession

Positive confession is one of the ways to give both yourself and your child hope. Positive confession or declaration is the practice of saying aloud what you want to happen, with the expectation that God will make it a reality. I am not talking about magic.

The verse in Proverbs 18:21 says, 'Death and life are in the power of the tongue'.

Many parents use negative words to their children without realising the impact and how it forms the blueprint for their future. I realised how powerful this was when I attended the T. Harv Eker boot camp, *7e Millionaire Mind*, realising the power of parents' words–usually not because of hate, but through ignorance of the powerful effects of words. Build your child's confidence! They need to believe in themselves, but instead they are told that they are stupid, an idiot, have no sense, ugly, a pain. Some parents find it difficult to speak encouraging words like, 'Well done for trying . . . next time will be better', or 'you are so beautiful or handsome', 'you are a blessing', 'I love you', or similar encouraging observations.

Whether you believe it or not, positive encouragement does make a big difference and should be preferred over constant criticism without giving any praise for effort or good behaviour. Such a situation has caused a lot of today's youths to give up and sometimes going as far as to join gangs, as they never heard the words of hope and encouragement that they needed. Instead, they were told and made to believe what a failure they are. Parents who find it difficult to release positive words should be aware that the wrong people are using this impact to take children away.

Gang members, for instance, tell such children how useful they can be and show them friendship and support. So when you tell your daughter how ugly and worthless she is, and that guy on the street showers her with words of love, telling her how beautiful she is, who do you think she will open up to? At the end of the day, you have no one to blame but yourself; you're only seeing and getting the results of what you've spoken. I urge you to read Joyce Meyer's wonderful book, *Change your Words, Change your Life*. Meyer goes into an in- depth discussion about the impact your words have on your life.

How many times have we heard that someone has died because of something they said in an argument? Consider the times when an unknown individual approaches you and says one kind word that changed your entire day! How many times has a word said by your boss, spouse, family, or friend caused you to feel so disappointed in yourself? How about when you've bought a piece of clothing you feel very excited about and after you're all dressed up with confidence, beaming in the mirror, you ask your partner, 'Honey, how do I look?' and the response is negative? You will quickly flip from feeling excited to feeling deflated, like a balloon whose air has been let out. I'm sure you can think up many examples and instances when words became true, so why would you think there is no power in what you say?

Remember, whatever you say, whether good or bad, will always release a reaction.

* * *

Imagine, then, the impact of negative words on a child who is still learning how to deal with all the different emotions and experiences of growing up. Remember, whatever you say, whether good or bad, will always release a reaction. It is for you to decide what response or reaction you want from your child before you speak, or what action you want from yourself–whatever you say is what you will do. If you say that you are going to fail automatically, subconsciously you have programmed failure into action. If someone wants to make you bitter or unhappy, they will say words to bring into being that reaction, just like the person who wants to get the opposite will choose cheerful words to make you feel excited, happy or encouraged. It's as if you are on a train. Never allow that engine to stutter or stop; though there are many carriages full of joy, laughter, tears, disappointment, hurt, failures, success, only you can determine what the last stop will be or what station you are going to.

Mindset

7e mind is everything. What you think you become.

I end this chapter discussing 'mindset', but you will find that it is the most important element of overcoming any form of challenge in your life. If you refuse to correct your mind-set, then you can forget trying to implement steps to take you to another level.

As I stated in an earlier chapter, no matter how many seminars or workshops you attend, until you have corrected your mindset you will remain the same; you will get all hyped up for that moment but will then go back to your old system of living. Your mind plays a crucial part of your transformation. When I say transformation, I am not talking about blinking and suddenly becoming a new person; I am talking about the process of pulling yourself from the depths to the elevation you have the potential to reach.

I remember when I was in my own prison with the wrong mindset, of which no one, not even I myself, was aware. I was not able to break free until I had corrected my mindset, the blueprint on which I was blindly building my life.

The mind is everything. What you think you become.

* * *

Until your eyes have been opened to where you are going wrong, as far as you are concerned, you are perfectly normal and consider yourself to be happy–which makes you settle for a mediocre life. I had to change my mindset in order to help my son, push to maximise my full potential and move away from the belief that other people in the world had decided to accept about their challenges. The great book instructs us, in Romans 12:2, 'Be not conformed to this world: But be ye transformed by the renewing of your mind…' In order to be transformed you need to renew your mind daily, removing the junk that the world will feed your mind and that will affect your progress.

When your mindset is governed by what everyone else around you is doing, then it will feed back to you exactly what everyone else is receiving.

* * *

When your mindset is governed by what everyone else around you is doing, then it will feed back to you exactly what everyone else is receiving. To ensure positive results your mind has to be fed with the right information. After my morning devotion, I make a point of listening to some of the world's greatest speakers such as Tony Robbins, Les Brown, Jim Rohn, Zig Ziglar, Nick Vujicic and many others, to ensure that my first hour of the day was feeding positivity to my mind. Challenge yourself to read at least one book per month that gives you knowledge about your current situation and where you want to be. Your mind is the machine of your life, and what you put in is what you get out.

Nothing is impossible; once you programme your mind to something, you can achieve it.

* * *

In order for you to become what you desire, you need to programme your mind to that success by envisioning yourself having already attained that goal. Your mind will eventually start accepting what you have programmed it to think and will push you to accomplish that vision.

Nothing is impossible; once you programme your mind to something, you can achieve it. Where or what is it that you want to achieve? What challenge are you facing that your environment and circumstances are telling you that you cannot overcome?

I urge you right now, as you are reading this book, to programme your mind to see success, feed your mind with positivity and surround yourself with successful people.

As the great Les Brown says, 'There is greatness within you'. Go forth and maximise your full potential: Overcome those challenges by turning the downside of your challenges into the upside of renewing your life.

SEE YOU ON TOP!

CONCLUSION

First, love yourself for who you are, and love your child for who he or she is. Don't try to change personalities. Then, correct your mindset and weed out the bad characters who will adversely affect the personality that makes you who you are. Parents, appreciate your children and bear in mind the fact that there are other parents facing worse situations than you are, so make the best of what you have. More importantly, for those of you reading this who have realised where you are going wrong, work on your weaknesses certainly, but focus on your strengths and you might be surprised as to what you have and what you can actually do. Overcoming the challenges you face also helps you to find out who you really are.

Don't be too proud to ask for help! For a long time I carried a chip on my shoulder, thinking everyone should know what I was going through and offer their unsolicited assistance. What an impractical assumption to make! I, too have cried myself to sleep many nights, so I know how it feels. But no matter what, do not give up hope or expect a miraculous, overnight transformation, which is where many of us often go wrong.

I know my journey has not yet finished; even as I am writing this book, greater challenges have shown up and other milestones have been overcome. Even so, I am comforted in knowing that once I have been able to succeed thus far, I can achieve and overcome a whole lot more. It's therefore fitting to leave you with this: If I can do it, so can you. You are no different, and though your situation may be different, it is not worse, as everyone's challenge is great to them.

Never settle for excuses and keep striving for the solutions you need: Give up and fail, or fight on and succeed. It is only you who can overcome and rise above what it is that you are battling with, which will enable you to turn the downside of your challenges into the upside of renewing your life.

End.

RESOURCES THE AUTHOR RECOMMENDS

1. MARKFIELD COMMUNITY CENTRE HARINGEY
   www.markfield.org.uk

2. WEBSTER STRATTON PROGRAMME
   www.tinyurl.com/carolynwebsterstratton

3. STRENGTHENING FAMILIES STRENGTHENING COMMUNITIES
   www.raceequalityfoundation.org.uk

4. ADHD KIDS
   www.adhdkids.org.uk

5. ADDISS – ADHD INFORMATION SERVICES
   www.addiss.co.uk

6. HYPERACTIVE CHILDREN SUPPORT GROUP
   www.hacsg.org.uk

7. WOMEN'S AID
   www.womensaid.org.uk

8. ADHD+SUPPORT
   www.adhd-support.org.uk

9. MARKFIELD COMMUNITY CENTRE HARINGEY
   www.markfield.org.uk

10. WEBSTER STRATTON PROGRAMME
    www.tinyurl.com/carolynwebsterstratton

11. STRENGTHENING FAMILIES STRENGTHENING COMMUNITIES
    www.raceequalityfoundation.org.uk

12. ADHD KIDS
    www.adhdkids.org.uk

13. ADDISS – ADHD INFORMATION SERVICES
    www.addiss.co.uk

14. HYPERACTIVE CHILDREN SUPPORT GROUP
    www.hacsg.org.uk

15. WOMEN'S AID
    www.womensaid.org.uk

16. ADHD+SUPPORT
    www.adhd-support.org.uk

17. PLACE2BE
    One of the leading UK providers of school-based emotional and mental health services, working in over 230 primary and secondary schools across the UK.
    www.place2be.org.uk

18. YOUNG MINDS
    www.youngminds.org.uk

19. HARINGEY INVOLVE
    www.haringeyinvolve.com

20. CAMHS – CHILD AND ADOLESCENT MENTAL HEALTH SERVICES (NHS)
    www.tinyurl.com/camhs-tier-3-team-haringey

21. IPSEA
    Independent Parental Special Education Advice
    www.ipsea.org.uk

ACKNOWLEDGEMENT

First, I must thank my Creator, the One who has made this book possible and given me the strength to make this exceptional testimony, The Almighty God, my Saviour.

Where do I start saying 'thank you' to the multitude of people who have touched my life? In no particular order, I'd like to express my gratitude to my grandparents Hazel and Clarence Sinclair, who raised me to be the woman I am today, and my grandparents Ashley and May Smith who have always been there for me. My mum Anita and dad Colin, without whom I would not be here; I'm eternally thankful for their constant guide, love and support.

I also salute those who are directly responsible for this book becoming a reality: My husband, Allain, who has loved me and been a devoted source of strength in raising our children; I could not have asked for a better husband. Many thanks to my beautiful and adorable children, Santana, Rashaun and Alisha, my gems of inspiration. You have never ceased to amaze me and put a smile on my face no matter the circumstances; the challenges you face are the keys that opened the door for this book, so be proud of yourselves in the knowledge that we are victorious and that I love you always for who you are.

Thank you to my brothers Dwayne, Jermaine, and Aaron and sister Serina. I thank each and every member of my family: If I were to state names I would never finish, but you've all been my listening ears, supported me when I went wrong or made bad choices, and helped with the mentoring and discipline of the children. The Sinclair and Smith families serve as my towers of strength; I could not accomplish all I have without you all. Thank you to my pastors, Peter and Julie Oyebobola, who taught me a lot of wisdom and opened me up to the idea of writing this book. God has used them to impact my life and I will be forever grateful. To Jackie, my child-minder: You've given me comfort in knowing I didn't have to worry about my children in your care.

To my ICCC family, the children's teachers: I've found a family in you all, which means a lot. Thank you for helping us fulfil our purpose, and giving your love and understanding to us. My neighbours, close friends, the staff of Devonshire Hill Primary School, Markfield Community Centre and CAMHS Burgoyne Rd, all the various groups that have been involved: Thank you. To my work colleagues who assisted me in my shift changes to attend meetings and emergency call outs, I thank you all. Thanks also to Ras Al for helping with this book; your knowledge, care and kindness have helped more than you know.

This book was only a dream, but by Gods grace it has been brought to reality. You all helped to make it happen, and words can never express the change you have made in my life and the future that is ahead of me. I want to thank you all for offering so many great ideas and training and answering my many questions at various hours of the day or night, which gave me the encouragement to go on: You are all awesome! THANK YOU ALL SO, MUCH!

BONUS CHAPTER
The Final Say

Your Current Situation is Not the Final Say

Throughout my journey, these past years, I have learned that life is full of unpredictable ups and downs. It is not uncommon to experience challenging circumstances that make us doubt our abilities and future prospects. During these moments of adversity, it is important to recognize that our current situation is not the final say on our lives. Regardless of our present circumstances, there is always room for growth, improvement, and the possibility of a brighter future.

As I reflect on my journey, I am astounded by the highs and lows that I have experienced. I never could have imagined the incredible successes that I have achieved. This book, which began as a way for me to share my story and offer support for others on a similar path, has become much more than that. It has been an incredible journey of self-discovery and accomplishment.

To give you a better understanding of my experiences, and to inspire you let me provide you with a glimpse into my life since writing the first edition of this book by sharing my bio with you and highlighting my achievements – this is not to brag but instead to make you know and understand that if I can do it, so can you.

My Bio

Michelle has done phenomenal work in growing her brand and dedicates herself to transforming the lives of many worldwide to go from being ordinary to extraordinary through the art of personal development, writing and speaking. Her numerous affiliations & recognition surround her passion for life transformation, motivation, vision creation and financial growth. Michelle's core passion is influencing individuals, families, entrepreneurs, and organizations to achieve their personal, financial, and entrepreneurial goals. She is a sought-after speaker and has worked with some very highly influential individuals to accelerate transformation and impact. Michelle has released 4 books including her bestseller *Overcome & Rise Above — How to Turn the Downside of Your Challenges into The Upside of Renewing Your Life,* followed by *Rise Above & Believe It's Do or Lie — How to Get Rid of Excuses & Create the Life You Desire. Authority — How to Write Your Book & Use It as A Marketing Tool for Your Business, Your Book & Beyond* as well as co-writing three other powerful books.

    Michelle is known as an inspiration with her open honesty, bold, bubbly yet powerful personality, that shines with passion and has motivated thousands all over the world, being an international speaker. She has been speaking for the past 10yrs and within this time has won numerous awards, received a letter of commendation from Her Majesty Queen Elizabeth reflecting her impact. After hearing Michelle Speak, her uplifting character, warmth, and humour will leave you challenged and inspired to take the actions necessary to bring about change. Michelle will show you how to break-free, believe and build to create the life and business you not only desire but deserve. She firstly began with her dedication to giving back to her community via her Women Be event which enabled women to break-free from their circumstances, believe in themselves & learn techniques on how to start a business & build a brand.

Michelle is an overcomer against all odds and teaches through her various seminars, masterclass, programmes and going into organisations to bring about transformation with her speaking and training modules. She is a wife, mother of three children and is the pure essence of success, born in London but raised from the age of 3 in the country of Jamaica. A survivor of domestic violence, from a previous marriage, suicidal tendencies, depression, huge financial debts and through the many challenges she has faced whilst parenting her son diagnosed with Special Needs, Michelle has taken the opportunity to turn her pain into a passion by sharing the experiences of her journey. Her insights and experience in life of overcoming difficulties has inspired many. Michelle strongly believes that your pain can become your passion, this passion has endowed her with abilities and strategies to help others overcome those stumbling blocks on their journey.

The numerous challenges this inspirational woman has faced propelled her to not only write her books but to also assist others to share their story and has created coaching programs that has helped to change the life of others. Michelle strongly believes that *"your life is a book, you cannot go back and tear out the pages already written but you can determine what is going to be written in the next chapter of your book called life."*

Notable Achievements

Spoken on stages/organisations such as
- The Women Economic Forum
- National Achievers Congress
- Power to Achieve (Amsterdam)
- Events for Champions (Thailand)
- Professional Speakers Academy (Dubai)
- The National Commercial Bank (Jamaica)

Featured On/In
- Sky TV
- Harold Hill radio
- Womelle Magazine
- Harvard Business Review Magazine
- London Live TV
- The Digging Deep Show
- Power Xtra Radio
- Stand Out Woman Radio
- Oasis Universal Radio

Awards / Honours Received
- Letter of commendation from Her Majesty the Queen (2017)
- Mentor of The Year (2018)
- Performance Coach of The Year (2020)
- Speaker of The Year (2017)
- Best Opening to a Presentation (2016)
- Global Authors Award (2018)
- Women Appreciating Women Awards (2020)
- Global Women Awards (2022)

Author
- *Overcome & Rise Above* (Bestseller)
- *Rise Above & Believe*
- *Authority*
- *Your Book & Beyond*

Co-Author
- Ordinary Women doing Extraordinary Things
- Les Brown Changed My Life
- Stories of Truth

Most requested speaking and training topics
- Developing healthy boundaries & a strong sense of self worth
- Influential Leadership
- Resilience & The Confidence Principle
- Mental Health & Suicidal Prevention
- Creating Content That Sells
- Developing The Mindset for Success
- Write to Become an Authority
- Domestic Abuse & Women Empowerment
- Teamwork in The Workplace
- How to Turn the Downside of Challenges to The Upside of Renewing Your Life

Whenever I read through my bio, it forces me to pause and reflect on my journey Looking back to when I embarked on this path, I could never have imagined the incredible opportunities and successes that lay ahead. At that time, I saw my starting point as my ending point and believed that was the limit of what I could achieve. However, as we are reminded in the Book of Job, that his "latter was greater than his past," and so can ours. This powerful message highlights the fact that our current circumstances do not have to dictate our future. Ultimately, we are in control of our destiny through the decisions we make and the steps we take. Over the years, I have discovered that certain steps have been critical in realising my goals and creating a brighter future. These steps have allowed me to recognise the potential for growth, even in the face of adversity. By embracing change, focusing on resilience, and taking ownership of my life and decisions, I have found a path forward that has been both fulfilling and rewarding.

I will share a few of these lessons with you

The Power of Perspective

Perspective plays a vital role in our perception of our current situation. It is easy to become caught up in the difficulties we are facing and lose sight of the potential for change and progress. Instead, try to shift your perspective towards a growth mindset. Understand that setbacks are temporary and can serve as valuable learning experiences. Believing that your current situation is not definitive allows you to embrace new opportunities and possibilities.

Embracing Change

Change is an inevitable part of life and can be tremendously empowering if we embrace it with an open mind. Rather than resisting change or feeling defeated by unforeseen circumstances, consider them as stepping stones to personal and professional growth. Embracing change requires flexibility, adaptability, and a willingness to explore new paths. Remember that change often leads to new opportunities and a chance to create a better future.

Learning from Challenges and Failures

Challenges and failures are not indicators of our worth or potential. Instead, they are opportunities for growth, resilience, and innovation. When faced with adversity, examine the lessons it offers. Reflect on the skills, knowledge, and strengths that you can gain from overcoming obstacles. Each challenge and failure are a chance to learn, adapt, and become better equipped for future successes.

Building Resilience

Resilience is the ability to bounce back from setbacks, and it is a crucial trait for navigating through life's challenges. Cultivating resilience enables you to persevere in the face of adversity, maintain a positive outlook, and keep moving forward despite obstacles. Understand that setbacks are part of the journey and that your ability to overcome them only strengthens your character and resilience.

Paving Your Own Path

While your current situation may feel limiting, it does not define your future. Take charge of your destiny by creating a vision for yourself and setting meaningful goals. By actively working towards your aspirations, you can take small steps each day that will lead to positive change and progress. Trust in your abilities and seize opportunities that align with your passions and values.

In conclusion I want you to remember that your current situation is not the final say on your life. By shifting your perspective, embracing change, learning from challenges, building resilience, and paving your own path, you can transform your circumstances and create a future filled with success and fulfilment. Believe in your capacity to grow, adapt, and overcome, and always remember that the best is yet to come.

I would like to encourage you to hold on to the hope that the best is yet to come. In the midst of challenges and uncertainties, it can be easy to lose sight of the possibilities that lie ahead. However, it is during these moments that we must remind ourselves that there is always potential for a brighter future. By nurturing a positive mindset and maintaining a belief in our own resilience and capabilities, we can navigate through difficult times with the knowledge that there are better days on the horizon. When we hold onto hope, we open ourselves up to the opportunities and possibilities that await us, fuelling our determination to strive for greatness and embrace the journey ahead.

I am eagerly looking forward to sharing more with you in my next book. Stay tuned and keep your eyes peeled for its release. On another note, if you have a story to share, I encourage you to no longer hesitate. There is someone out there who is in need of hearing your story. Your experiences and insights can make a positive impact on others, so embrace the opportunity to share and inspire.

> *"A story not shared, is a message not heard and a life not saved."*
>
> — *Michelle Watson*

* * *

BREAKFREE FOREVER CONSULTANCY

Michelle Watson
SPEAKER | MENTOR | AUTHOR

Overcome & Rise Above: How To Turn The Downside Of Challenges Into The Upside Of Renewing Your Life

NEED HELP TO SOLVE THOSE CHALLENGING SITUATIONS?
LOOKING FOR A SPEAKER TO MOTIVATE & DRIVE YOUR TEAM?
ARE YOU IN NEED OF A PERSONAL DEVELOPMENT OR BUSINESS COACH?

For further information to attend a motivational seminar or workshop to empower women, please contact:
Email: *michellewatson@breakfreemw.com*
Phone number: +44 7578 990 16

www.ingramcontent.com/pod-product-compliance
Lightning Source LLC
Chambersburg PA
CBHW042117100526
44587CB00025B/4087